Pans with a smooth internal surface area, straight sides, and also level bottom are liked. Hefty graniteware or porcelain-lined pots are excellent for candy making. Iron utensils are not encouraged for steaming sugar as they are most likely to discolor the candy. Light weight aluminum pots are generally also slim as well as hand out way too much heat completely sweet making. Remember that kettles ought to be big sufficient to permit the candy to boil without outraging. Because of this, good heavy kettles are needed. For ease, the words "pot" or "double central heating boiler" will certainly be made use of throughout this program. Constantly add water in reduced fifty percent of double central heating boiler. MARBLE SLAB
To appropriately deal with as well as cool your candy syrup, it is a good idea to have a smooth marble slab. The marble slab should be at least 1 1/2 inches thick to prevent the slab from breaking because of the hot sweet syrup. You can acquire this sort of product from a supply home that deals in sweet making, or from your local marble and tile electrical outlet. Steel, sheet iron, or a concrete slab may satisfy likewise, however marble is preferred. Make sure the piece is level when in operation so the hot sweet syrup will not run off the edges.

When making tiny batches (for instance, when you are experimenting), you may use huge china platters to cool your candy syrup. For ease, the word "slab" will be utilized throughout this training course.
Butter, olive oil, or any type of great food preparation oil may be utilized on the piece so candy will certainly not stick. No oil is required when making supply or lotion sweets.
IRON BARS
For additional aid, area steel bars, concerning 3/4" x 3/4" square, the size of the piece to assist avoid sweet syrup from running off.
CONFECTIONER'S THERMOMETER
Effective sweet making depends a lot on properly steaming sugar as well as regulating the temperature level to the proper degree, depending on the type of sweet being made. It is an excellent suggestion, when about to use your

thermometer, to place it near the oven or some other slightly cozy area in the cooking area prior to making use of.

SPOONS
Aheavy spoon or spatula is made use of for creaming sweet syrup. The tool should be made from hardwood or steel. It is suggested that you have a long, twisted piece of cable with a loop on the end for dipping sweet as well as making such things as bon bons.

STARCH TRAYS
Here are 2 good ways to make molds for lotion candies. One is by hand as well as the other 1 is by using starch trays. Starch trays are normally 13" x 25" or 18" x 36" in size, as well as can be supplied by a confectioners' supply home. The trays need to be loaded with corn starch or molding starch, and kept completely dry.

WAFER-LINED TRAY
Wafer-lined tray may be either a tin tray or wood starch tray lined with French or german wafer. Any type of great confectioners' supply residence need to be able to equip this wafer, which comes in packs of 100 sheets.

FUNNEL
The channel is made use of for running the thawed cream stock right into the starch impressions. It is additionally 1 used for going down cream supply wafer or patties.

CANDY HOOK.
This product is typically offered via confectioners' supply homes. Anchor it to something strong, such as your kitchen wall. To "pull" little sets, you might use just your hands.

ACTIVE INGREDIENTS.
Sugar may be bought at your local shop.

Cream of Tartar is utilized with sugar to stop granulation, and also might be acquired at your neighborhood shop. Take care not to use excessive.

Colors and also Flavorings-- Besides the ones you make yourself, you might acquire these items at your confectioners' supply home.

Paraffin Substitute-- One kind is kokoreka. Another is difficult nut butter (such as palm kernel or cocoa butter or oil). Examine your confectioners' supply residence.

VITAL CANDY MAKING ESSENTIALS COOKING WITH AN OPEN FLAME.

When using an open flame such as on a gas range, the warmth or fire need to be kept low enough to stop the flame from rising the sides of the kettle and also shedding any kind of sugar that may have adhered to its sides. When this kind of heat is made use of, the fire must cover the entire base of the pot so that there is even warm circulation.

PROTECTING AGAINST CRYSTALLIZATION.

As you are preparing the sweet syrup, make sure to keep the inside walls of the pot spick-and-span. You can do this with a wet cloth or sponge. This eliminates any grains of sugar that could stay with the sides of your utensil. They would certainly start a crystal development when your candy is being put or defeated if you were to let these sugar granules to remain. It would certainly be sensible, additionally, not to scratch the saucepan as you pour the candy. This, also, might start.
a crystal formation.

MIXING OR WHIPPING CANDY.

Such things as sea foam or divinity are composed mostly of egg whites and also steaming syrup, and also are stiffly defeated to blend in air to consider that light cosy structure. Take great care when adding the boiling syrup, making sure you do.

Really gradually so the air that you mixed in earlier will certainly not escape. When the boiling syrup is put with the.
beaten egg white, it heats up and also cooks the egg white.

TEMPERATURE-TESTING SWEET.

You need to understand the temperature level of your sweet to recognize what stage it is in. Use either a confectioner's thermostat or the cool water approach. The bulb of the thermostat must be entirely inside the boiling candy syrup, yet should not touch the frying pan at any type of time while attempting to obtain a proper reading.

Use a little cup or container filled with cool water. Put about 1/2 t. boiling sweet syrup right into the cool water, then choose up the candy in your fingers to test the uniformity.

There are 4 major types of sweet you will certainly be examining for:.

Soft Ball-- The candy will certainly create a soft round however will rapidly lose its form when drawn from the water. Hard Round-- The candy will hold its shape a little longer prior to ending up being really soft once again.

Soft Crack-- The sweet develops brittle threads in the water and afterwards softens when eliminated from the water.

Hard Split-- The sweet will develop breakable threads, as with soft crack, but remain brittle when gotten rid of from the water.

When examining these candies with a thermostat, seek the list below temperature levels for certain stages of sweet.

Usage great treatment when steaming syrup to a high level. As well much warm might scorch the sugar prior to the thermostat has a possibility to sign up properly.

The same boiling degree is utilized whether making little or huge batches.

Sweet syrup containing corn syrup will certainly burn a lot more swiftly than that containing straight sugar and cream of tartar. Sugar and cream of tartar can be steamed to 330 ° F with proper warmth.

When making little sets it is often challenging to get the thermostat to go deeply sufficient into the syrup to sign up properly; you might need to rely upon the chilly water test up until you take place to bigger amounts. NUT

CANDIES.

Best outcomes on nut sweet of any kind will certainly be acquired on days that are dry as well as cool. Cozy weather will certainly trigger the candy to come to be sticky and run. It needs to be positioned in waxed paper-lined pails or sealed boxes if candy is to be kept for any kind of length of time.

MAKING DESIGNING ICING Solution 1:.

Soak overnight 4 ozs. flaked albumen in 11/2 pints water. Mix and also defeat, slowly adding and also functioning in 6-7 Ibs. Confectioner's sugar. Beat until really light.

Formula 2:.

Another simple recipe for icing is to beat 3 egg white up until frothy. Stiffen by working in confectioner's sugar till regarding the density of corn syrup. Use baker's rubber ornamenting bag for embellishing. If icing is too thick to lack bag, thin with a little water (not way too much).

MAKING HOLLOW DELICIOUS CHOCOLATE NUMBERS.

In dual central heating boiler, melt great quality sweet delicious chocolate. Prepare as for covering cream. Area mold and mildew in amazing room and permit to set.

MAKING CHOCOLATE NUT BARS WITH METAL MOLDS.

Location in cold place to cool before making use of. Prepare delicious chocolate as for layer cream facilities, using an excellent grade sweet or milk delicious chocolate. Place a couple of handfuls of dissolved delicious chocolate on piece as well as mix and blend completely with fingers.

to cool to touch. With huge spoon, fill up each area of metal mold structure. Location in great area to harden. Faucet mold and mildews gently to get rid of bars. Wrap in tinfoil.

MAKING HARD CANDY.

A copper kettle is favored for this work, but a thick-bottomed, graniteware pot may be made use of. Usage tool warm as well as watch syrup so it does not scorch. Prepare difficult candy as swiftly as feasible without burning. Piece ought to be tepid.

PREP WORK FOR STARCH MOLDING.

If making use of starch trays filled up with corn starch, board should be a dimension in percentage with starch tray dimension. Glue mold and mildews to board, then established in the starch trays. Enable enough space between each mold so that there will certainly be starch around the edges of each impact when the impressions are loaded with sweet syrup.

ABBREVIATIONS.

The following abbreviations and also close variations will be utilized throughout this training course.

C. = cup sq. = square Ib. = extra pound T. =tbsp oz.

MISCELLANEOUS SWEET IDEAS CONFECTIONERS' SUPPLY RESIDENCES.

In this modern of ours it is a reasonably simple thing to browse the net, under the heading of sweet making confectioners or products supply residence, to discover an excellent provider for your candy making requirements.

Your public library might likewise have phonebook from throughout the nation that can inform you the local confectioners' supply home available to you.

SAVING CANDY.

Do not use iron or aluminum. Rather, use traditional candy storage.

containers such as stoneware, dishware, or graniteware. You might likewise use stainless-steel, high-temp glasses, or ceramic.

Fudge-- Leave in pan and cover tightly with foil, to keep velvety and soft. Location in an awesome, completely dry place.

Sugar-- Cover each piece independently in cling wrap, allowing sweet show with. Shop in covered container.

Make right into rolls and also location in plastic bags, maintaining the lumps, or rolls, in entire type, to aid maintain moist. Might be cooled to make slicing much easier when all set to make use of.

SENDING BY MAIL CANDY.

Good selections to mail, which travel well, are fudge, caramels, or fruit drops. Use metal container as well as area a layer of smashed waxed paper in base. Cut dividers of cardboard and fit into box to maintain pieces from moving. After organizing sweet attractively in container, add cover and tape, or tie container closed, for added protection. Area container in extremely solid, bigger container or container, and fill in rooms with smashed paper or various other sorts of mailing supporting to protect from declines or bounces. Cover outer container in great covering paper. Connect firmly and also affix tag to carton. Mark on plan that warmth will certainly harm contents.

STANDARD SWEET FOUNDATION: LOTION SUPPLY OR FONDANT.

Cream supply or fondant is the basic structure of all cream candies.
Again, when making little batches you might have an issue utilizing the thermostat considering that the thermostat will not be able to go deeply enough right into the sweet to register accurately. While steaming the syrup, do not to mix, move, or container the kettle being made use of. This might begin the granulation of the candy, causing it to come to be tough.
Lotion of tartar is used to "grease" the sugar and prevent formation, however do not make use of way too much or it will certainly avoid your sweet from creaming.

effectively. Supply made of sugar as well as cream of tartar produces a very creamy smooth cream and is the purest. Egg whites or gelatin might be added to stock or fondant in order to make it much more soft and velvety.
Lesson 2 CREAMING PROCEDURE.
The warm syrup has to remain in the creamed phase before it awaits use. Moisten a flawlessly clean.
Marble piece with cold water. Pour hot syrup onto piece. Keep in mind not to scratch all-time low of the kettle; this might take shape the entire batch. Sprinkle a few handfuls of chilly water over the warm syrup so a crust will not develop.
When awesome, stir with wood paddle or steel spatula, transforming over and over many times, thoroughly functioning the syrup. Proceed to mix and also defeat for about fifteen mins, until blend sets into a company lump of pure white lotion. Do this as you would massage bread, till set becomes soft and luscious.
Superior creamed sweets are made from stock that has had time to mellow or age. In this method you might utilize a heavy spatula or other utensil, and be able to use your arms rather of your wrists.

SPECIAL NOTE: Ought to syrup that is currently cream, begin to have large crystals, or start to transform or granulate right into sugar, becoming as well hard to knead, place batch into water and also liquify back to original stage. Never add any kind of lotion of tartar or glucose to a batch that is being re-boiled unless adding much more sugar. Any kind of lotion of tartar included need to be in proportion to the amount of sugar added.

Make sure the slab is level when in usage so the warm sweet syrup will not run off the sides.

Successful candy making depends a lot on properly boiling sugar as well as controling the temperature level to the suitable degree, depending on the kind of sweet being made. Aheavy spoon or spatula is made use of for creaming sweet syrup. Put about 1/2 t. boiling sweet syrup right into the cold water, after that select up the candy in your fingers to examine the consistency.

Again, when making small batches you may have an issue utilizing the thermostat since the thermostat will certainly not be able to go deeply sufficient into the candy to sign up properly.

CREAMSTOCKNO.1(PLAINCREAMSTOCK)

In kettle, place 5 Ibs. Sugar, ½ t. cream tartar, and one qt. water. Stir on stove until thoroughly dissolved. When boiling, carefully skim off any foreign material. Cover kettle (a wooden cover is preferable) and allow the syrup to boil another 2 or 3 minutes. Remove cover and. thoroughly wash down the inside walls of the kettle. Place thermometer, which has been slightly warmed by lying near the stove, into the boiling syrup and allow to

remain there until it registers 238°F. When this degree has been reached, instantly remove kettle from stove and pour mixture onto a perfectly clean slab which has been slightly dampened with water. Sprinkle small amount water over the hot candy syrup to cool and ready for the creaming process. You will be instructed how to make a smaller batch of this fondant in the exercise section.

CREAM STOCK NO. 2

In kettle, place 3 Ibs. sugar and 1 pint water. Stir on stove until thoroughly dissolved. Boil to 240°F. Pour onto a clean, damp slab and allow to cool. Sprinkle 1/2 t. cream of tartar over mixture, turning in the edges, and work until soft, white, and creamy. Cover with damp cloth for half an hour, then knead with your hands and store away in a stone jar.

Lesson 3

CREAM MELTING PROCESS
Good centers for bon bons depend greatly on the melting of the cream stock to the correct temperature. Place a quantity of your stock in a double boiler or a kettle set inside another, and partly fill with water. (Do not attempt to heat or melt stock without using a double boiler. No matter how good your stock is, too much heat will ruin it.) Place on stove and add desired color and flavorings. Stir constantly, using as little heat as possible, until of a thick cream consistency. Never allow stock, at this point, to boil, as this will make it lose its creamy soft texture. When the stock is properly melted, the center should be as butter.

Lesson 4
MOLDING CREAM CANDIES
The best way to mold cream candies, such as bon bons, etc., is by hand or in starch. Usually, if one tries to use solid molds, the cream becomes so hard that the candy is very poor for eating. Cream centers molded in starch remain soft longer than do solid molded cream centers.

When starting starch work, fill starch tray with a good grade fine, dry corn or potato starch which is free of lumps. Pack starch tightly in tray, and smooth off to surface level with ruler or flat stick. Press plaster of Paris molds lightly into the starch and remove. Molds will leave impressions in the starch, ready for melted stock. Use confectioner's funnel to fill impressions. By raising and lowering funnel stick, fill each impression. Set aside the filled

to allow the centers to harden. When hard, gently lift centers off trays with spoon. Gently dust off excess starch that may stick to hardened cream center. (If too much starch sticks to the centers, this could mean cream was poured too cold when poured into trays, or that starch was damp. Do all starch work in a warm, dry room.) Centers are now ready for dipping.

CREAM DIPPING PROCESS
Dipping your cream centers gives them a professional look. Dipping stock should be boiled a bit higher than cream centers stock.

Boil dipping stock to 240°F-242°F. For the most part, it is good to use cream stock to which you have added cream of tartar because this produces a firmer coating and gives your bon bons more gloss. Melt the cream the same as previously learned. You may make centers one day and coating the next.

If your cream is too thick, thin by adding water.

Melted cream that is hot enough for dipping should read 139°F on your thermometer. Hold wire candy dipper in right hand. With left hand, drop hardened centers, one at a time, into melted stock. Before center softens, quickly take out with dipper. Carefully scrape off excess coating on side of kettle. Place coated centers on waxed paper to harden.

Coating which runs down the sides of centers indicates it has been thinned too much, or that stock was too soft-boiled, sometimes due to poor grade of sugar.

VANILLA BON BONS

In double boiler, melt down a quantity of cream stock that has a percentage of corn syrup. Flavor with vanilla to taste. Run stock through funnel into starch impressions. Allow to harden, and then dip in the plain stock. Set aside on waxed paper to harden again.

LEMON BON BONS

Follow the same steps as for vanilla bon bons, using good grade lemon extract and yellow coloring.

PINEAPPLE BON BONS

Use pineapple extract and no coloring

STRAWBERRY BON BONS

Use strawberry extract and a light red coloring. Other bon bons can be made using the same general instructions.

Lesson 6 HAND MOLDING BON BONS

All bon bons may be made by hand. Add flavor and color as desired to cream stock. Work and knead with the hands until soft and creamy. Use a small amount of confectioner's sugar to make cream firm enough for molding and to prevent sticking to hands. Mold into small ball, pyramids, or other shapes. Place on waxed paper to harden. When hardened, bon bons are ready to be dipped.

SOFT CREAM STOCK

In kettle, place 12 1/2 lbs. granulated sugar, 2 1/2 lbs. corn syrup, and 3 pints of water. Dissolve thoroughly. Cover kettle and allow to steam for a few minutes. Dampen marble slab during this time. Remove kettle cover and place thermometer well into syrup. Boil to about 240°F. Carefully remove kettle from stove. Pour hot syrup onto damp slab. Allow to cool, then cream.

Cover with a heavy cloth and set aside to age or condition.

In another kettle, place 2 lbs. sugar, 1 lb. corn syrup, and 1 pint water. Stir on stove to dissolve thoroughly. Boil to about 242°F. Remove kettle from stove. Add 2 1/2 ozs. sheet gelatin previously dissolved in 1/2 pint hot water. Cream with a paddle or egg beater until thick and creamy. In double boiler, melt down first batch, now under cloth. Add second batch during melting.

Melt slowly, using as little heat as possible, to produce a very fine, soft cream center. Run into starch impressions. Allow to harden overnight. Remove and dust off excess starch. Dip in plain melted stock.

Lesson 8
ITALIAN CREAM STOCK
In kettle, place 10 lbs. sugar with enough water to thoroughly dissolve. Add 1/2 t. cream of tartar, stirring well. Boil to about 246°F. Add 4 ozs. pure glycerin and continue to boil to 246°F. Pour onto damp slab. When lukewarm, add well-beaten whites of six medium-sized eggs. Cream with paddle to produce an excellent creamy center, used mainly for Italian chocolate creams or old-fashioned chocolate drops.

Lesson 9
MAPLE CREAM STOCK
In kettle, place 3 lbs. sugar with enough water, about 1 1/2 pints, to make thin syrup when dissolved. Stir on stove to dissolve. Strain into another kettle. Add white sugar and 3/4 lb. corn syrup. Dissolve and boil to about 240°F. Pour onto clean slab and sprinkle with water. When lukewarm, cream.

Store in crockery or stoneware, and cover with heavy cloth until ready to use.

Lesson 10
IMITATION MAPLE STOCK
Imitation maple stock is made by using plain brown sugar instead of maple sugar. Follow general cream stock instructions for maple cream stock. May be made without corn syrup by substituting
¾ t. cream of tartar. Cream of tartar is preferable when used for dipping.

CHEAP CREAM STOCK
In kettle, place 5 Ibs. granulated sugar, 1 Ib. corn syrup, and 1 1/2 pints water. Dissolve on stove. Cover kettle and allow to steam for two or three minutes. Dampen marble slab at this time. Remove the cover and wash inside walls of kettle. When beginning to boil, place thermometer in syrup and cook to 240°F. Pour onto cool, damp slab. When lukewarm, cream. SPECIAL NOTE: When melting this stock to be run into starch impressions, add 1/2 to 3/4 Ib. corn syrup. Stir well into melting cream.
Lesson 12
HAND-ROLLED CREAM RON RONS NUT CREAM BON RONS
To 5 Ibs. cream stock, add 2 oz. butter, 1 t. vanilla extract, and 1/2 Ib. chopped nuts of any kind. (English walnuts or pecans are the best.) With hands, knead nuts and butter well into stock. Use a little confectioner's sugar to make stiff. Mold into balls, oblongs, or other shapes. Place on waxed paper in a dry, cool place to harden. When hardened, dip one at a time in melted cream stock. Set on waxed paper to harden again.
ORANGE CREAM BON BONS
To 5 Ibs. cream stock, add grated rind of 1 orange and 1 t. orange extract. Knead and mold mixture as for nut cream bon bons.
RASPBERRY CREAM BON BONS
To 5 Ibs. cream stock, add 1/2 Ib. finely chopped almonds and }/2 t. almond extract. Mold as with other hand-rolled cream bon bons.
BUTTER CREAM BON BONS
To 5 Ibs. cream stock, add good quality creamery butter and 1 t. vanilla extract. Knead well into the cream stock. Place mixture in cool, dry place (such as a refrigerator) for a short time. Mold as with any other hand-rolled cream bon bon. Make sure this very rich type of candy does not become to warm or it will become rancid after a short time.
COFFEE CREAM BON BONS
To 5 Ibs. cream stock, add 1 T. good coffee extract. Proceed as with other hand-rolled creamed bon bons.
Lesson 13 **SUPER FINE CREAM STOCK**
In kettle, place 5 Ibs. sugar with almost 1 qt. water. Stir on stove until well

dissolved. Add about ½ t. cream of tartar. Cover kettle and allow to steam for two or three minutes. Dampen marble slab at this time. Remove kettle cover and wash down inside walls of kettle. Boil mixture to about 242°F. Pour onto damp slab. When batch is lukewarm, add on top of batch the beaten whites of two or three eggs. Cream with a paddle or spatula.
This stock may also be used for hand-molded bon bons and makes a delicious soft cream. Divide batch into two or three pieces, and flavor and color to taste. Mold by hand into pyramids, balls, or other shapes, and place on waxed paper to harden. Dip in melted cream stock. If desired, top off with nuts right after dipping in melted cream stock.

Lesson 14
MEXICAN PECANOLA
In kettle, place 3 Ibs. brown sugar with 1 pint fresh cream. Stir until thoroughly dissolved. Bring to boil and place thermometer in syrup. Stir very gently, and do not use too high a heat. Cook to 238°F. Immediately remove kettle from stove and allow batch to cool about 4 or 5 minutes. At that time, add 1 to 11/2 Ibs. shelled pecan halves and 1 oz. butter. Beat vigorously until very smooth and creamy. Use spoon or fork to drop out onto heavy waxed paper. Shape into little kisses, or, if preferred, into cakes or patties. If candy becomes too stiff to spoon out, soften by putting in a double boiler and melting down as you would stock or fondant. For less expensive candy, use condensed milk instead of cream and walnuts instead of pecans.

Lesson 15
CREAM WAFERS
In clean kettle, place 5 Ibs. sugar and 1 qt. water. Dissolve on stove. When at a boil, skim off all foreign matter which comes to the top. Wash down inside walls of kettle. Cover and allow to steam for 2 or 3 minutes. At this time, sprinkle slab well. Remove kettle cover and place thermometer in syrup. Boil to 242°F. Do not stir during boiling or mixture may start to

granulate. If necessary, add 1 t. cream of tartar to help prevent granulation; however, mixture is usually better without it.
Carefully pour batch onto well-sprinkled slab. Leave for short time, then sprinkle lightly with cold water and allow to become lukewarm. Cream with paddle or spatula. Store in stone jar or crock and keep covered with a damp cloth.

This formula makes a very good cream wafer. In double boiler, place 2- 3 lbs. cream in double boiler and stir thoroughly, using very low heat until warm enough that you do not burn your finger when you put it in the cream. If cream is too hot, wafers will spot; if not hot enough, they will stick together. During the melting process, use any flavor or color desired. Do not lay waxed paper on a cold slab as this will also spot the candy. Put waxed paper on table or starch trays. Fill funnel about 2/3 full melted cream. If cream is too thick to pour into funnel, add a little cold water and stir until hot again. Run cream through funnel onto waxed paper, forming small round wafers. Allow to harden. Turn waxed paper so that wafers are upside down. Lightly pull waxed paper off, leaving wafers to harden even more.

CREAMED DIPPED NUTS

In double boiler, place quantity of plain cream stock. Stir on stove until it becomes like thick cream. Hold wire candy dipper in right hand. With left hand, drop English walnuts, pecans, almonds, hazel nuts or other type nuts into cream. Quickly turn over and lift out with wire candy dipper. Place one at a time on waxed paper. If too much heat has been used in melting process, cream may run off nuts. Add a little confectioner's sugar to help with this problem. If cream is too stiff, place back on stove and stir until it reaches desired thickness.

Lesson 17

mixture is at melting stage,

CREAM NUT PATTIES

In double boiler, place quantity of plain cream stock. When generously drop nut pieces in kettle and mix thoroughly. Spoon mixture onto waxed paper. Allow to harden. Different type nuts create many varieties of this candy.

Lesson 18 DIVINITY KISSES

In kettle, place 2 lbs. sugar, 4 oz. corn syrup, and 1/2 pint water. Boil on stove until thoroughly dissolved. Boil to 246°F. Slowly add 1 C. heavy, fresh cream. Stir continually to prevent scorching. Boil to 238°F. Remove kettle from stove and pour contents onto cool, damp slab. Sprinkle hot syrup with a little water to prevent mixture from forming crust. On top of batch, add egg white beaten to froth. Allow batch to cool, then cream with paddle or spatula. Place in double boiler. Using low heat, allow water to boil. Stir cream stock until melted enough to spoon out. Add 1/4 lb. walnut or pecan halves and 1 oz. butter. Flavor lightly with maple. With spoon, cut into patties or kisses, and place on waxed paper. Substitute evaporated milk for the cream and use a more commercial type of nut, if desired.

Lesson.19 MAPLENUT-INES

In kettle, place 1 Ib. brown sugar, 1 Ib. maple sugar, and 1/2 pint water. Stir on stove until thoroughly dissolved. Wash down inside walls of kettle. Boil to 238°F. Meanwhile, beat well 1 egg white and add a small amount vanilla. When batch has reached correct degree, remove from stove and add 1 t. butter. Allow batch to cool until just warm to touch. Place beaten egg and vanilla in large kettle. Pour syrup over beaten egg, remembering to stir very quickly until creamy and stiff. Add nuts while stirring, if desired. With greased spoon, drop small amounts on waxed paper to harden. If mixture becomes too hard to spoon out, place in double boiler and melt a little, as with cream stock cream.

SEA FOAM KISSES

In kettle, place 2 Ibs. Add 1/4 t. cream of tartar. Boil to 238 ° F. Remove from stove and add 1 t. butter.
Spoon onto waxed paper as well as enable to solidify.

Lesson 21 SAUERKRAUT SWEET

In kettle, place 1/2 Ib. Allow to boil, then add 1 1/2 oz. While boiling, have on hand a cup of cold water so as to perform the cold water testing method.

pot from oven and also add small amount salt. Place in the amount of coconut syrup will certainly cover. Include 1 drop lemon essence while including coconut. Put components onto gently oiled piece and also permit to cool down. Cut into shapes as you prefer.

Lesson 22 PEANUT-INES

In pot, place 2 Ibs. sugar, 1/2 Ib. corn syrup, 1/4 C. molasses, and 3/4 pint water. Mix on oven up until extensively liquified, after that add 1 oz. butter. Add 3 t. bicarbonate of soda and mix into batch. Add 3/4 Ib. Place on greased marble slab.
Lesson 23

CREAMED ENGLISH WALNUTS
Shell an amount of English walnuts, maintaining each fifty percent of nut whole. Knead a quantity of stock lotion until creamy and soft. Enclose half a walnut in small amount of stock, shaping as desired.

CREAMED PECANS
Proceed when it comes to creamed English walnuts, utilizing pecans as opposed to English walnuts.

CREAMED HAZEL NUTS
Knead hazel nuts into an amount of cream stock. ALMOND CREAM BON RONS
Prepare almonds by shelling and also getting rid of internal skins. Do this by submersing in hot water for a couple of minutes. Split in half, lengthwise, as well as permit to dry. Roast in oven until brown. Knead a quantity of lotion stock until soft as well as velvety. Type stock right into forms about the length of almond fifty percents. Put on waxed paper and allow to set. Dip in dissolved supply. Position an almond half on each shape and once again leave on waxed paper to set.

Lesson 25

LOTION NUT ROLL
Divide a quantity of supply into three parts and add desired quantity of flavor. Shade one component red, an additional brownish or chocolate, as well as leave the third white. Forming each part into sizes of around 6" -8" long and also 1" -2" wide. Area busted nut items over top of white supply. Location red supply in addition to this as well as

Place brown stock on top of red. Place on waxed paper to harden. If planning to keep for some time, dip in melted cream stock.

Lesson.26 CREAM POTATOES
Form an amount of cream stock into pieces about the size of small potatoes. If desired, put shredded coconut into holes.

Lesson 27 CHEAP FUDGE
In kettle, place 3 Ibs. Boil to 240 ° F. Remove kettle from stove and add 1 1/2 Ibs. Allow syrup to cool for a few minutes, then thoroughly cream and work with paddle or spatula.

Lesson.28 LOTION FUDGE
In kettle, place 3 Ibs. sugar, 1 Ib. corn syrup, as well as 3 pints wonderful cream.
Add 2 Ibs. Let cool for a few minutes, then mix or cream into smooth, creamy fudge. If desired, add shredded coconut, chopped nuts, or fruit.

DELICIOUS CHOCOLATE FUDGE
In kettle, location 21/2 Ibs. sugar, 1 Ib. corn syrup, 1 pint evaporated milk, and also 11/2 ozs. paraffin alternative or hard nut butter. Stir constantly to avoid scorching. Prepare to 238 ° F. Include 8 ozs. grated bitter delicious chocolate. Get rid of kettle from oven and add 1 Ib. smooth cream supply. Permit to cool. Flavor with 1 t. vanilla. Beat or cream swiftly till gloomy in look. If desired, add nuts. Pour onto tray or pan lined with waxed paper. A wood frying pan is preferred. Score into squares. When cold, squares may be broken apart.

Lesson 30 AFFINITY KISSES

In kettle, area 3 Ibs. sugar, 1 pint water, and also 1/4 t. cream of tartar and also liquify completely. Boil to 240 ° F. Dampen marble piece. Put mix onto wetted piece. Great to lukewarm, after that put 2 completely beaten egg whites over set. Add 3/4 Ib. pecans, in items. Cream till thick, like cream supply. Allow sit for a while, covered with a towel, after that melt in double boiler. Spoon onto waxed paper to make kisses. Wrap in waxed paper.

Lesson 31 COCONUT-LEMON KISSES
In kettle, place 31/2 Ibs. Spread with3/4 Ib. Cream, then cover with cloth for short time.

Lesson 32 COCONUT LOTION BAR
In kettle, place 31/2 Ibs. sugar, 1 Ib. corn syrup, and 1 pint water. Mix up until extensively liquified. Boil to about 238 ° F. Eliminate kettle from oven. Add 4 Ibs. cream stock. Mix till velvety. Add 11/2 Ibs. shredded coconut and also vanilla to preference. Pour contents in between iron bars (see "Iron Night clubs," page 4) onto waxed paper. Enable to cool down. Cut into bars concerning 11/2" wide as well as 31/2" long.

SPECIAL NOTE: If batch becomes too solid after including supply, place in double boiler to soften.

Make Strawberry Coconut Cream Bars by tinting lotion pink as well as flavoring with strawberry. Make Chocolate Coconut Lotion Bars by

adding 1/2 lb. grated bitter chocolate to cream stock.
COCONUT CREAM BON BONS
To three parts kneaded and flavored cream stock, add two parts fresh grated coconut. When hard, dip into melted stock.

Lesson 34 FRENCH COCONUT CREAMS
In kettle, place 3 lbs. Dissolve on stove and add 1/4 t. cream of tartar. Cream.

Use several flavors as well as shades to make variations of this candy.

Lesson 35 COCONUT ROLLS
Knead a quantity of cream supply till creamy and soft, adding taste and shade as preferred. Kind into wanted forms as well as leave on waxed paper to set, or until at least firm enough to manage. Melt a percentage of lotion stock and place in meal. Spread shredded coconut in one more dish. Roll solidified lotion shapes in melted cream, then in coconut, until completely covered. Place on waxed paper to cool, completely dry, and harden.

Lesson 36 CREAMED DATES
Load facilities of pitted days with flavored and tinted stock. Dip packed days in melted supply and put on waxed paper to solidify.

Lesson 37 CREAMED FIGS
Add small pinch cream of tartar. Dip into melted stock,
using flavor and shade preferred.

Lesson 38 FRENCH CREAMED STOCK
Whip six egg whites up until frothy as well as rigid. Beat in 1/2 C. gum arabic water (see listed below). Operate in enough confectioner's sugar to make flexible and firm. French supply can not be melted like steamed supply, and also have to be molded by hand. Form into wanted forms. Usage stock immediately considering that it quickly comes to be difficult. For a finished appearance, dip into dissolved lotion supply.

GUM ARABIC WATER-- Gum tissue arable water may be made by soaking 4 ozs. white powdered periodontal arabic in 1/2 pint boiling water. Stir as well as dissolve thoroughly. Stress and allot for use. Bigger quantities may be made by using proportionately larger amounts.

Lesson 39 COCONUT BISCUIT

In a dish, gradually mix 1/2 C. confectioner's sugar, 1/2 C. sifted flour, 1/2 C. corn syrup, and two egg whites, defeated well. Work in 4 C. shredded coconut. Decline mixture onto greased frying pan or baking sheet and also place in moderate stove for 15 mins.

Lesson.40.
FRENCH NOUGAT.

In kettle, place 4 Ibs. Cream mixture very thoroughly. Add 1 1/2 Ibs.

Lesson 41.
TUTTI-FRUTTI NOUGAT.

In pot, area 5 Ibs. sugar, 4 Ibs. corn syrup, 2 ozs. paraffin alternative, as well as 1 qt. water. Dissolve extensively. Boil to concerning 260 ° F. Allow to cool down for about 4 mins. Beat 9 egg whites till frothy and stiff. Pour cooled down syrup over egg whites, stirring intensely, flavoring lightly with vanilla. Beat till tight, working in 1/4 Ib. candied cherries, 1/2 Ib. walnuts, and 1/2 Ib. candied or polished pineapple. Lotion well as well as pour into wafer-lined box or tray (see "Unique Note," Lesson 40). Push down with board. Permit to set over night. If preferred.

Lesson 42.
MAKING DELICIOUS CHOCOLATE SWEET.

Coating chocolate may be purchased from any confectioners' supply house. Ordinary baker's chocolate may be used, and will serve the purpose nicely for many classes of candies.

TEMPERATUREFORCOATINGCHOCOLATE.

Even if your chocolate is of the best quality, it will not hold up against summer heat or a warm store room. Do not allow your candy to come in contact with ice, or allow it to remain in the refrigerator too long, as it will spoil.

Lesson 43.
HAND-COATING CHOCOLATE CREAMS.

When you melt chocolate, use a double boiler to keep chocolate from direct heat. Mix and blend, then drop hardened cream centers into chocolate with your left hand, one at a time. With the right hand, roll the cream centers

around and coat.
Lesson 44.
DIPPING CHOCOLATE.
In double boiler, melt a quantity of chocolate until liquid enough to drop cream centers into. Stir thoroughly into chocolate to avoid streaking. Drop cream centers, one at a time, into mixture with left hand.
Lesson 45.
CHOCOLATE PEANUT COLLECTIONS.
In a double boiler, thaw an amount of sweet chocolate coating. Put onto marble piece. Job and also blend with hands. Permit to cool on the slab. When chilly to the touch, dip Spanish roasted peanuts right into coating. Make clusters of about 6 nuts each. Set on waxed paper to harden.
Lesson 46 BITTERSWEETS.
Mold centers of Italian or superfine stock and coat with bitter chocolate. Use different shapes and flavors, as desired. Make with nut centers or top with nuts.
CHOCOLATE MARSHMALLOWS.
Dip marshmallows into an amount of sweet chocolate, as in coating bon bons.
Lesson 48.

Cream until thick, like cream stock. Make Strawberry Coconut Cream Bars by coloring cream pink and flavoring with strawberry. Make Chocolate Coconut Cream Bars by adding1/2 Ib. Roll hardened cream shapes in melted cream, then in coconut, until thoroughly coated. In double boiler, melt a quantity of chocolate until liquid enough to drop cream centers into.
CHOCOLATE BAR
In dual central heating boiler, melt 3 Ibs. plain cream stock. In one more double central heating boiler, melt1/2 Ib. bitter chocolate. Mix together with 2 ozs when both are melted. butter. Mix well with paddle or spatula. Pour1/2" thick onto tray or frying pan lined with waxed paper. Enable to cool down, then cut into bars 4" long and 1" broad.
To make nut bars, include English walnuts, pecans, or peanuts when mixing lotion and also chocolate.
Lesson 49

CHOCOLATE BON BONS
In double central heating boiler, thaw an amount of lotion supply made with corn syrup, utilizing tastes and shades as wanted. Run through funnel right into starch impacts. Permit to set. Get rid of from perceptions, cleaning off excess starch. Layer with thawed delicious chocolate.

Many different sort of chocolate bon bons might be made by doing this. These bon bons might likewise be made by hand. Taste as well as color cream stock as desired. (Usage vanilla, lemon, strawberry, pineapple, orange, banana, climbed essence, as well as various other flavorings, tinting as necessary.) Usage small amount of confectioner's sugar to make tight. Build into other forms or small balls.

Position on waxed paper to set. Layer with chocolate.

Lesson 50

CHOCOLATE ALMOND CREAMS
Add flavoring as wanted. Dip into dissolved delicious chocolate and also area in great area to solidify.

Lesson 51

CHOCOLATE PEPPER MINT CREAMS
In double boiler, thaw lotion stock. Add simply enough pepper mint to provide a great, abundant taste. Go through funnel, dropping in tiny rounded patties or cakes onto heavy waxed paper. Permit to solidify enough to deal with. Coat with wonderful delicious chocolate. These creams might additionally be molded in starch delicious chocolate COCONUT BALLS Knead a quantity of lotion supply with hands until soft as well as velvety. Taste as wanted. Shape right into spheres the dimension of little marbles and also put on waxed paper to harden. Forming right into balls the dimension of tiny marbles and also area

on waxed paper to solidify. Place an amount of coconut on flat dish. Thaw a quantity of wonderful delicious chocolate as well as place on an additional recipe. Dip set cream spheres into delicious chocolate until well-coated. Roll in coconut while covering is still soft. Reserve on waxed paper to solidify.

Lesson 53

DELICIOUS CHOCOLATE COCONUT BON BONS
Include enough newly grated coconut to cream stock to make smooth paste, using a little confectioner's sugar to avoid sticking. Place on wax paper to set.
Lesson 54
CHOCOLATE NUT PATTIES
In one pot, melt 2-3 lbs. In one more kettle, melt 1 lb. When both are thawed, blend with each other, stirring in damaged pieces of nuts of selection.
MEXICAN KISSES
In pot, area 1 lb. Stir on cooktop up until extensively dissolved. Include 1 1/2 lbs.
Lesson 56
DELICIOUS CHOCOLATE COVERED CHERRIES
Roll well-drained maraschino cherries into confectioner's sugar and permit to dry momentarily, then dip in warm, dissolved lotion stock (to create crust which will, to some extent, avoid juice from escaping the fruit). Put on waxed paper and allow to solidify. Layer with wonderful or bitter delicious chocolate and enable to solidify. Cover in gold or tin foil. These ought to keep for time.
AFTER DINNER MINTS
In kettle, location 4 pounds. Stir materials till extensively dissolved. Location 1/2 lb. smooth, simple cream supply in the facility of set. Fold up in edges

with candy scrape or knife. When great enough to take care of, place on sweet hook to draw. Do not place sweet on hook when as well hot, or sweet might slip off hook. While pulling, add 1 T. peppermint remove for flavor. Draw candy on hook till white in color. Dirt counter or table with confectioner's sugar. Remove sweet from hook as well as position on counter or table. Form into bottle shape, and rotate or draw out in rope-like style. With hefty shears, clip sweet rope right into lumps concerning 1" long. Allow to establish overnight.
Pack into air-tight containers. ^

Lesson 58 CHOCOLATE CHIPS
In pot, location 4 Ibs. When great enough to deal with, area on candy hook. Place close to range or set warmer to maintain soft qualities.

Lesson 59 PERIODONTAL DROPS
Liquify 4 ozs. granulated jelly in 11/2 pints warm water as well as reserved. In kettle, area 3 3/4 Ibs. granulated sugar, 2 Ibs. corn syrup, and concerning 1/2 glass water. Stir constantly up until syrup boils. Cook to 240 ° F. Remove kettle from cooktop and also enable to cool around 3 minutes. Include prepared gelatin water as well as mix well. Color as well as flavor as preferred. Run into really dry, warm starch impressions. Sort a little starch over molds as well as leave in impacts for 2 or 3 days. When getting rid of the centers, dirt off and crystallize to complete. If wanted, wet gum decreases and also roll in granulated sugar.

Lesson 60 MARSHMALLOWS
Liquify 3 1/2 ozs. granulated jelly in 1 pint warm water as well as reserved. In pot, location 4 Ibs. sugar, 3 Ibs. corn syrup, and 1 qt. water. Mix on oven to thoroughly dissolve. Boil to 240 ° F. Remove from range and also permit to cool for 1 min. Add ready gelatin water. Beat and mix mixture vigorously with

paddle Or spatula up until it has consistency of ruined egg whites. (The more you defeat the mixture, the lighter and far better the ended up item will certainly be.) Dust marble slab with corn starch, to prevent sticking. Pour set onto piece. Permit to establish, and then cut in 1" squares.

MAKING TAFFIES AND TOUGH SWEET
Treatment should be taken when making candies that need a high steaming temperature level.

Molasses is graded according to its sugar content. Utilize the best molasses. Prevent making use of molasses dark, substandard molasses, as it will certainly not cook up effectively. Stir continuously to stop scorching or boiling over.

Lesson 62 MOLASSES SPONGE CHEWING TAFFY
In kettle, place 2 qts. When cool sufficient to deal with, location on candy hook and also pull up until light and also mushy. Include 1
When extensively drawn, flatten on table which has actually been dusted with a little corn starch. Pull or spin taffy into strips regarding 3" wide.

SPECIAL MOLASSES TAFFY
In pot, place 5 Ibs. Stir on stove up until completely dissolved. Boil to 254 ° F. Add 1 qt.
Lesson 64
PREMIUM MOLASSES PEPPERMINT TAFFY
Liquify 1 level t. granulated jelly in Vs glass warm water as well as reserved. In pot, location 2 1/2 lbs. sugar, 2 1/2 pounds. corn syrup, 1 pint top quality molasses, and 1/2 pint fresh lotion. Stir on oven till thoroughly liquified. Boil to 246 ° F. Include 3 ozs. butter. Continue to steam to 254 ° F, then eliminate

Pour onto amazing, greased slab. Sprinkle jelly water over top of syrup as well as fold in edges. When great enough to deal with, location on candy hook.
MOLASSES KISSES
In a kettle, place 21/2 Ibs. of sugar, 21/2 Ibs. corn syrup, 2 ozs. chocolate butter, and also 1 pint fresh lotion. Stir on oven to thoroughly liquify. Boil to 250 ° F. Include 1 C. of top quality light molasses and 1 T. butter. Boil to 254 ° F-258 ° F.(If making this candy in cozy weather, the higher temperature is chosen.) Put onto a greased slab and also permit to cool down. When trendy enough to take care of, place on sweet hook. Flavor to taste with vanilla while pulling.
Roll into rope-type shape on a table that has been lightly dusted with corn starch. Cut, or clip with shears, right into kisses about 1" long as well as around as thick as finger. Cover in waxed kiss paper.
Lesson 66
PEANUT BRITTLE
In a kettle, location 3 Ibs. Boil to regarding 240 ° F. Include 2-21/2 Ibs. Prepare until peanuts have well-roasted scent and syrup is gold yellow in shade.
Usage chilly water examination. Combination checked will certainly become really weak, like an egg covering. Get rid of from oven. Include 2 t. bicarbonate of soft drink as well as 1/2 t. table salt. Pour onto cozy, greased piece and also spread as very finely as possible. Turn set upside-down, seeing to it spreads out as very finely as in the past. When cool, rating candy as well as burglarize pieces. Pack in waxed paper. Maintain in cool,

completely dry location to prevent from becoming sticky.
PEANUT-COCONUT BRITTLE
In pot, place 3 Ibs. sugar, 2 Ibs. corn syrup, and also 1 pint water. Mix on cooktop to extensively liquify. Boil to 240 ° F. Include 2 Ibs. Spanish peanuts.
Remain to steam and mix. Add all the chip or thread coconut syrup will take in when peanuts are cooking well and syrup has actually become golden in shade. Include 1/2 t. salt, 1 t. bicarbonate of soda, and also 1 small item butter. Mix and work well with paddle or hefty spatula. Put onto greased slab. Spread

very finely. When cool, disintegrate and stack items in pans. Pack in waxed paper and also shop in awesome, dry place.
Lesson 68
WALNUT BRITTLE
In pot, area 3 Ibs. sugar, 2 Ibs. corn syrup, and also 1 pint water. Stir on stove to completely liquify. Boil to regarding 256 ° F. Add regarding 1 1/2 Ibs. black walnuts. Stir well and steam to 290 ° F, or to hard fracture stage. Add 1 t. salt. Pour onto greased slab. Spread thinly as feasible.
When amazing, turn set upside-down, making sure it spreads out as thinly as before. After cool, break apart and cover in waxed paper. Store in trendy, completely dry place.
Lesson 69
ALMOND BARS
In a pot, place 4 Ibs. sugar, 2 Ibs. corn syrup, as well as 1 1/2 pints water. Stir on range to completely liquify. Boil to 240 ° F. Include 3-3 1/2 Ibs. shelled almonds, mixing in gradually. Remain to mix and steam components up until almonds are brownish and syrup is brittle when checked in chilly water. Put onto greased slab between 2 iron bars (see "Iron Bars," page4) When cool, reduced right into 2 oz. bars.
Lesson 70
MAKING CARAMELS
When sugar are made properly, they are soft and also crunchy. You might have steamed the syrup too long when sugar become difficult and also weak. Stir continuously to prevent scorching. Constantly make use of the finest wonderful lotion. You may use a good warm when beginning to steam the

set, but minimize warmth as batch obtains done.

Delicious chocolate caramels may be made by utilizing any of the adhering to solutions and adding 1/2 Ib. Nut sugar are made by adding sliced walnuts, pecans, or almonds. Stir in nuts after eliminating pot from the cooktop.

FRENCH SUGAR

In a kettle, area 2 Ibs. sugar, 2 Ibs. corn syrup, 1 1/2 pints fresh light cream, and also 1 pint compressed milk. Dissolve completely on oven, mixing continuously to stop scorching. Prepare to the difficult ball phase or to 246 ° F. Remove from oven. Add 2 ozs. carefully shaved paraffin replacement. Flavor with

2 T. vanilla. Mix well as well as put onto a chilly, greased slab.

Lesson 72

COSTS SUGAR

In pot, area 3 Ibs. sugar, 3 Ibs. corn syrup, 1 qt. lotion or condensed milk, and 3 ozs. paraffin alternative. Mix on range to extensively liquify. Boil to regarding 248 ° F, mixing constantly. Put onto cool, greased piece. Permit to cool down up until lukewarm, and also place 3/4 -1 Ib. smooth lotion supply on set. Knead with hands up until smooth. Cool at wanted thickness on piece which has iron bars on each side. Reduced right into sugar dimension items when batch is entirely cooled. This is an excellent hot weather sugar and also will certainly not promptly become stale.

Lesson 73

SUPERFINE CARAMELS

In pot, area 2 Ibs. Boil to soft sphere stage, or 244 ° F. Include 1/2 pint much more cream and also once more steam to soft ball phase. Taste with 1 t. vanilla as well as put onto a cold, greased slab, between the iron bars or in tins, regarding 1" in depth.

EXPENSIVE PEANUT BARS.

In kettle, location 2 1/2 Ibs. sugar, 1 1/2 Ibs. Corn syrup as well as 1 pint water.

Boil to concerning 238 ° F. Add 3 Ibs. Syrup must be brittle when evaluated in chilly water. Remove from oven as well as include 1 t. salt.

CRYSTALLIZING.

Business suppliers take shape a big quantity of their candies. If preferred, you may crystallize your candies to provide a completed, expert look. An excellent, glossy, ended up look is really.

appealing, specifically in summer months, as well as will certainly stand up well. It is tough to delicious chocolate layer throughout very warm climate unless effectively equipped. You will require a syrup gauge, or, as it is likewise understood, a saccharometer. You will additionally need a quantity of taking shape frying pans. These are normally about 21/2" deep and have a detachable cord grate or screen which fits down right into them. You will likewise need a gauging tin or holder to utilize with your saccharometer. A confectioners' supply home can provide you with these products.

You might place your scale into water to check the scale's precision. Do not utilize if gauge signs up anything besides absolutely no.

Boil syrup up until your saccharometer registers 331/2. Usage saccharometer on syrup to check for details gravity. Boil syrup as rapidly as possible.

Test when syrup starts to steam by scooping out a tin full as well as putting saccharometer right into it. The saccharometer will certainly increase to leading. Enable to drift, as it were, in syrup. When it signs up at the factor where the gauge and syrup satisfy, this will be the right level.

Meticulously pour syrup over facilities up until they are completely immersed, or to a depth of 1" or so. Allow centers to stay under syrup for 14 hrs. By manages at each side of cord grate, lift grate out slowly, enabling syrup to drain back.

If syrup does not have actually glossy taken shape look or finish, syrup has not boiled at a high enough temperature level, with the outcomes being also rugged a crystal.

Make use of a routine confectioner's thermostat to steam the syrup if you do not have a syrup gauge or saccharometer. To get crystal syrup of 33 Vi, boil sugar and also water to 228 ° F, after that add a quantity of water to lower temperature level to 226 ° F. Let cool down to 106 degrees. Pour syrup over centers, as defined above.

Crystallize cream wafers by making use of the above instructions.

Crystallize almond lotions by dipping the facilities in crystal syrup instead of dissolved lotion supply. Crystallize packed dates in a 34 F crystal syrup.

Stir continuously till syrup boils. When peanuts are cooking well and syrup has actually come to be golden in color, add all the chip or thread coconut syrup will take in. Proceed to stir as well as boil materials until almonds are brownish and also syrup is breakable when checked in chilly water. Examination when syrup begins to boil by scooping out a tin complete and putting saccharometer into it. If you do not have a syrup gauge or saccharometer, utilize a normal confectioner's thermostat to steam the syrup. Include 1/4 t. Lotion of tartar. Melt in double boiler, including 1/2 Ib. Spoon into cream kisses onto hefty waxed paper.

LESSON 76
WHAT A LITTLE EXPERIENCE CONTAINER DO
After a little experience, you will have the ability to make many of your very own initial kinds of candy.
CHOCOLATECREAMSQUARES
Cut cream stock into 1" squares, 1/2" thick. Dip in melted pleasant delicious chocolate and also position on waxed paper to solidify in cool, dry area. Usage different tastes and also colors in lotion stock to produce large selection of squares.
COCONUT BALLS
Job a quantity of dry coconut right into lotion supply as well as form right into spheres the size of huge marbles. Coat rounds with delicious chocolate rather of lotion stock.
CREAM NUT SQUARES
These resemble nut rolls. Cut into small squares and also dip in dissolved stock. Make chocolate nut squares by dipping in delicious chocolate rather than cream supply. Usage various flavors and also colors for huge assortment of squares.
JELLY ROLLS
Proceed as for cream nut rolls, yet as opposed to nuts in between the lotion

stock, use hefty jelly. Cut right into small squares and crystallize, utilizing taking shape directions. Make chocolate jelly squares by dipping in chocolate rather than crystallizing.

CREAM BALLS
Kind balls of lotion stock, concerning the size of huge marbles, as well as crystallize, utilizing different colors and tastes.

CHOCOLATE DROPS
Make large pyramids of lotion supply. Allow to solidify. Coat with pleasant chocolate.

Lesson 77 EVERTON TOFFEE
Boil rapidly to 290 ° F. Stir sometimes while steaming, to avoid scorching. Cook to 290 ° F. Add 1/2 Ib. Remove from range as well as add a couple of decreases lemon flavor.
While still warm, mark off right into squares. When cold, break apart and also cover in heavy waxed paper.

BUTTERSCOTCH
In pot, location 3 Ibs. Boil to 286 ° F. Include 4 ozs. Taste with a couple of declines strong lemon and 1 t. table salt.

GOODY-NUT KISSES
In pot, place 2 1/2 Ibs. sugar, 2 1/2 Ibs. corn syrup, and 1 pint water.
Bring to boil. Include 2 ozs. Cover set around peanut butter.

Lesson 80 YELLOW JACK
In pot, place 3 Ibs. sugar, 2 Ibs. corn syrup, 1 pint premium light molasses, and 1 pint water. Mix on cooktop till extensively liquified. Offer steam. Add 2 ozs. butter and also 4 ozs. paraffin replacement. Mix regularly as well as cook to 264 ° F. Pour onto cold, greased piece as well as fold in sides. When cool sufficient to handle, put on sweet hook and draw up until really light. Squash on table lightly dusted with corn starch. Pull into 3" vast strips and also reduce right into 4 1/2" sizes. Wrap in hefty waxed paper.

WORKOUTS
EXERCISES FOR SOFT BALL CANDY (or 238 ° F)
. Workout 1-- Delicious Chocolate Fudge 2 C. sugar.
2 sqs. grated, unsweetened delicious chocolate.
1 t. vanilla2/3 C. milk.
2 T. butter or butter Vs t. salt replacement.
In pot, incorporate sugar, milk, butter, salt, and grated delicious chocolate. Boil to 238 ° F. Include vanilla and also allow to cool. When lukewarm,

defeat up until velvety and thick. Spoon onto wax paper or into shallow greased frying pan. Cut right into squares. Exercise 2-- Chocolate Honey Fudge.

2 C. sugar.

2 sqs. grated, bitter delicious chocolate.

2/3 C. evaporated milk 1/4 C. honey Vs t. salt 1 t. vanilla 2 T. butter.

In pot, location honey and also milk. Mix on cooktop to thoroughly liquify. Include grated delicious chocolate, butter, and also salt. Mix thoroughly. Boil to 238 ° F. Enable to cool up until warm. Add vanilla and defeat till luscious and also thick, as well as rigid adequate to hold form when spooned onto waxed paper.

Workout 3-- Peanut Butter Fudge 1 C. sugar Vs t. salt.

2 T. butter 1/4 Ib. peanut butter.

1t. vanilla 1 C. brown sugar.

In pot, integrate sugar, salt, butter, and milk. Boil.

1/2 C. vaporized milk 1 C. marshmallows.

to 238 ° F, or soft ball stage. Add marshmallows and peanut butter. Without mixing mix, eliminate pot from cooktop. Permit combination to cool.

till lukewarm. Add vanilla and defeat till creamy as well as thick, and also stiff sufficient to hold shape when spooned out. Put right into well-greased pan.

Exercise 4-- Peanut Honey Fudge 4 C. sugar.

2egg whites, stiffly defeated.

1C. peanuts (unsalted) Vs t. salt 1/2 C. peanut butter 1 C. water 1 t. vanilla 1. C. honey (stretched).

In kettle, place 1 C. sugar and 1/2 C. water. Boil to soft sphere phase, or regarding 238 ° F. Pour extremely gradually over ruined egg whites, mixing continuously until tight. In one more pot, place honey, peanut butter, 1/2 C. water, and also staying 3 C. sugar. Boil to 238 ° F. Slowly contribute to very first set, stirring frequently until stiff adequate to hold shape when spooned out. Include peanuts and vanilla. Go down does onto waxed paper.

Workout 5-- Delicious Chocolate Nut Raisin Fudge 2 T. butter 1/2 C. evaporated milk.

2C. sugar 2 sqs. delicious chocolate.

1/4 C. quality molasses 2 T. raisins.
In kettle, location sugar, milk, molasses, chocolate, as well as 1/2 C. cut nuts 1 t. vanilla.
thawed butter. Slowly warmth until delicious chocolate is extensively thawed. Boil to soft ball stage, or 238 ° F. Remove from cooktop and allow to cool till warm. Stir intensely up until luscious. Include raisins, nuts, and vanilla, as well as mix completely. Pour into shallow, greased pan.
Workout 6-- Penuche 2 C. brownish sugar.
1/2 C. cream.
2 T. butter 5 T. chopped dates 5 T. coconut 5 T. cut nuts.
In pot, location butter, lotion, and sugar. Boil to 238 ° F. Eliminate from cooktop and permit to cool down up until warm. Beat until velvety. Include dates, nuts, and coconut. Beat till thick. Put right into superficial, well-greased pan, and cut into squares.
Exercise 7-- Maple Nut Balls.
2 C. maple syrup 2/3 C. chopped nuts 1 t. vanilla 2 T. butter 1/8 t. salt.
Boil to 238 ° F. Eliminate from cooktop and also cool until lukewarm. Add butter and also vanilla.

creamy. Include half the nuts and continue to stir up until mix can be built right into little rounds. Roll balls in staying nuts as well as put on waxed paper to set.
Exercise 8-- Pecan Roll.
2 C. sugar 1 C. cream 1 C. light brown sugar 1/2 C. corn syrup 11/2 C. pecans In pot, place cream, corn syrup, as well as sugar. Boil to 238 ° F. Allow to.
great until warm, then defeat strongly till creamy. Put on board well-.
Knead with hands as well as shape into roll. A lot more nuts might be added during working, if desired. Establish apart to harden as well as cool.
Exercise 9-- Pecan Pralines.
1 C. light brown sugar 1 T. butter 1/3 C. of water 1 C. sugar 1/2 Ib. sliced pecans.
In pot, place sugar, water, and butter, as well as rapidly offer steam. Add pecans. Continue to boil, stirring frequently up until mix begins to bubble well. Eliminate from oven. Spoon onto greased marble slab.
Exercise 10-- Heavenly Hash 2 C. sugar.

1 t. butter.
1/2 cup roasted almonds 2 T. marshmallow lotion.
1 t. vanilla.
1C. lotion.
1/2 C. sliced pecans (approximate 20 to 25) 4 T. grated, unsweetened delicious chocolate.
21/2 C. marshmallows.
In kettle, incorporate chocolate as well as sugar, after that add butter and cream. Boil to 238 ° F. Get rid of from cooktop. Include marshmallow cream, nuts, as well as vanilla.
Stir till thickens. Put mix over marshmallows.
Exercise 11-- Gumdrops.
2T. gelatin 2 C. sugar 1/2 C. cold water 3/4 C. boiling water.
Thoroughly liquify gelatin in chilly water. In kettle, incorporate boiling water and sugar. Boil regarding 15 mins, after that take off warm. After 3 mins, thoroughly stir in jelly water. Divide set right into three equal components. Shade as well as taste as preferred. Put right into superficial frying pans which have actually been dipped.

Cut right into squares as well as roll in powdered sugar. Permit to solidify.

EXERCISES FOR HARD BALL CANDY (or 248 ° F)

. Workout 1-- Caramels.
2 C. sugar 13/4 C. corn syrup 2 C. cream 1 C. butter.
In pot, combine all ingredients other than nuts as well as continuing to be cream and boil to 248 ° F, or hard sphere stage. Include nuts.
Vs t. salt.
1 C. sliced nuts.
Boil concerning 30 mins. Include Exercise 2-- Sea Foam.
2C. sugar 1/2 C. water 1/2 t. vanilla.
2 egg whites 1/8 t. salt 1/8 t. lotion of tartar.
In kettle, area sugar, water, salt, as well as cream of tartar. Boil about 5 minutes, being sure to clean inside wall surfaces of pot with wet towel. Boil to tough sphere phase, or 248 ° F. Pour gradually over ruined egg whites, stirring frequently. Add vanilla. Beat till firm when gone down from teaspoon. Drop onto waxed paper. If desired, sprinkle with coconut.
Workout 3-- Divinity.

2 C. sugar 1 C. chopped nuts 1/2 t. vanilla 1 1/2 C. corn syrup 1/2 C. water 1/8 t. cream of tartar 2 egg whites, stiffly defeated 1/8 t. salt.
In kettle, location sugar, syrup, water, salt, and lotion of tartar. Boil concerning 5 mins, maintaining inside walls of pot tidy with wet fabric. Boil to 248 ° F. Eliminate from stove. Pour slowly over ruined egg whites, constantly stirring. When gone down from a teaspoon, beat till company. Include vanilla as well as nuts. Stop by teaspoonful to waxed paper, or, if preferred, pour right into superficial, wellgreased pan and reduce into wanted dimensions.

WORKOUTS FOR SPLIT SWEET (or around 270 ° F)Exercise 1-- Molasses Taffy.

1 C. molasses 1/8 t. salt 1 T. butter 2 t. vinegar 3/4 C. sugar 1/8 t. baking soda In kettle, place molasses, sugar, as well as vinegar. Boil to break phase, or.
270 ° F. Remove from cooktop. Add butter, baking soda, and salt. Mix gently.
sufficient to mix components. Put into a wellgreased frying pan. When amazing enough, pull (with hook or hands) till light and also airy.

Exercise 2-- French Taffy.
5 C. sugar 1 C. sweet lotion 2/3 C. warm water desired flavoring.
In kettle, location sugar and warm water. Gradually include lotion, mixing constantly. Boil to fracture phase, or 270 ° F. Include vanilla or various other preferred flavoring.
Exercise 3-Salt Water Taffy.
1 C. sugar 1/8 t. salt 2/3 C. honey 3 T. corn starch 1/2 C. water.
*.
In pot, combine sugar, corn starch, and salt. Add water and also honey. Prepare to 270 ° F. Pour into greased pan. When amazing enough, pull (with hook or hands) till light as well as permeable. Cut right into 1" pieces.
Exercise 4-Walnut Taffy 2 C. sugar.
1 T. butter.
1/2 C. sweetened condensed milk.
1/8 t. salt 1 t. vanilla 1/2 C. chopped walnuts 1/2 C. water 1 C. molasses.
In pot, incorporate molasses, sugar, butter, water, and salt. Boil to break phase, or 270 ° F. Include vanilla. Spread walnuts over bottom of superficial,

greased pan. Pour taffy over walnuts. When trendy sufficient, pull (with hook or hands) until stiff as well as luscious. Cut into 1" items.

EXERCISES FOR DIFFICULT CRACK CANDY (or 290 ° F).

Exercise 1-- Cracker Jack.

1C. molasses 1 T. butter, thawed 1/8 t. salt 1 C. sugar 3 qts. popped corn In pot, place sugar, salt, molasses, as well as melted butter. Boil to difficult split stage, or 290 ° F. Pour over snacks. Stir well while pouring. Spread in slim layer to cool. Burglarize items.

Workout 2-- Peanut Brittle.

2C. sugar 1/8 t. salt 1 C. peanuts 1 T. butter 1/2 t. baking soda.

In kettle, chef sugar, stirring regularly, up until a gold brown syrup is developed. Get rid of quickly from oven. Include salt, cut peanuts, cooking soda, and also butter. Mix to mix active ingredients. Pour swiftly into thin sheet in a superficial, greased frying pan. When cool, cut or get into preferred pieces.

Include 1/4 t. Cream of tartar. Taste with a couple of decreases strong lemon and also 1 t. table salt. In pot, location 1 C. sugar and 1/2 C. water. In another pot, place honey, peanut butter, 1/ 2 C. water, and also remaining 3 C. sugar. In kettle, incorporate chocolate and sugar, then add butter as well as cream.

CANDY COURSE ELECTIVES
Lesson 81
HOMEMADE FLAVORINGS

SPECIAL NOTE: Wood alcohol is deadly poison, but cologne spirits is an alcohol free from flavor, with good strength, and is good for use in making homemade flavorings.

VANILLA FLAVORING

Break 2 oz. pure vanilla beans into pieces. Place pieces in wide-mouthed bottle or jar. Pour 1 pint cologne spirits (alcohol) over vanilla beans. Cork tightly. Shake contents at least twice a day for a week or longer. Filter liquid through coffee filter into another jar or bottle. Liquid is ready for use. Always keep well-sealed with cork. Makes very strong flavoring which may be toned down to taste by adding a small amount of distilled water.

LEMON EXTRACT

Peel off yellow rind of 5 or 6 lemons. Put rind pieces in quart-sized wide-mouthed jar or bottle. Fill with cologne spirits (alcohol). Cork tightly. Shake a few times daily for a week or longer. Filter liquid through coffee filter into another jar or bottle. Liquid is ready for use. Always keep wellsealed with cork.

ORANGE EXTRACT

Place peelings from about 5 oranges in a jar or bottle of cologne spirits (alcohol). Use a larger jar than for lemon extract, as more alcohol is needed to absorb essential oils from orange peelings. Cork jar, then shake a few times a day for about a week. Filter through coffee filter into another jar or bottle.
Liquid is ready to use. Always keep well-sealed with cork.

COFFEE FLAVORING

Place two thicknesses of cheese cloth over mouth of bowl. Press cheese cloth into bowl, making an open bag. Pour 4 ozs. finely ground mocha coffee into bag. Pour boiling water over the coffee. After the water has passed once through the bag, take the same water and pour over again. Squeeze out the extract.

ADVANCED WORK IN CANDY MAKING
Lesson 82
CREAM STOCK OR FONDANT

To attain the best results in making fondant, corn syrup is a necessity. Fondant or cream stock made with just straight sugar will dry out quickly, especially when used in starch impressions. This is true especially with cream bars and cakes.

It is also important to use a type of agent to "grease," as it were, the batch to prevent the granulation of the syrup when cooking. Cream of tartar, acetic acid, fruit juices, and corn syrup are some agents used for this purpose. Some of these agents are better and easier to use than others.

A cream of tartar batch will require very careful supervision. The inside walls of the kettle should be washed down periodically to prevent sugar crystals from forming, resulting in grainy stock. A corn syrup batch will not require as much supervision and will not granulate as soon as batches made with other agents.

The fondant, made with cream of tartar or acetic acid, is usually used for dipping and coating purposes, such as with bon bons, or for running cream wafer. This type of cream stock or fondant is also good for fudges and nougats.

Care is needed when using these acids. If too much is used, your batch will be hard to cream or beat, and will likely be sticky.

Always cook syrup as quickly as possible without scorching. Allow to cool until lukewarm before proceeding with creaming process. If you try to cream when syrup is too hot, stock will be dry. It is good not to make too large a batch without the right equipment. Cream stock or fondant will keep a while if properly covered and protected, but do not wait too long before using it.

Lesson 83 CHOCOLATE WORK

When working with chocolate, room temperature should be 68°F or lower, never higher. When heating chocolate, use a double boiler or chocolate warmer. Grate or break up chocolate so it can melt quickly and easily. Stir constantly while melting.

When chocolate is entirely melted, take several large handfuls and place on marble slab. Work and mix well with fingers of right hand. The chocolate must be worked and mixed until well blended. Never coat any centers or bars until chocolate feels slightly cool to the touch. When chocolate is cool enough and thoroughly mixed, take in your left hand the candy centers to be coated and place in the center of chocolate. Coat and remove with right hand. Set coated centers and bars on waxed paper to harden. Waxed paper-lined wooden trays are good for this purpose.

Cool candy as soon as possible to ensure quick setting-up. As the chocolate on marble slab is used, replenish "chocolate bed," as it is sometimes called, from double boiler. Again, mix well with your right hand and allow to cool before coating centers.
If, at the time of coating, coating chocolate is too thick, thin by adding cocoa butter or paraffin substitute, remembering that too much will result in grayness and streaking.

In warm weather, work chocolate in cool, dry place. Keep chocolate dipped candies in cool place such as refrigerator. Never place on ice since this will cause a dull appearance. In some cases, it may be necessary to use a candy hardener such as coconut butter.

FORMULAS FOR CREAM STOCK
FORMULA I

n kettle, place 5 Ibs. sugar, 1 Ib. corn syrup, and 1 1/2 pints water. Stir on stove to thoroughly dissolve. Bring to boil, skimming off any foreign matter that rises to top. Boil to 238°F. Pour hot syrup on cold, damp slab.
Sprinkle a few handfuls water over surface of syrup to prevent crust from forming. When cool, cream into fondant.

FORMULA II

In kettle, place 5 Ibs. sugar, $1/4$ t. cream of tartar, and 1 1/4 pints water. Stir on stove to thoroughly dissolve. Bring to boil, skimming off any foreign matter that rises to top. Boil to 240°F. Add 1 Ib. corn syrup and again boil to 240°F. Pour onto cold, damp marble slab. Cream when cool.

FORMULA III

In kettle, place 4 Ibs. sugar, 1 Ib. corn syrup, and $1 1/4$ pints water. Stir on stove until thoroughly dissolved. Bring to boil, skimming off foreign matter that rises to the top. Boil to 238°F. Pour on damp, cold marble slab. Cream when cool.

FORMULA IV

In kettle, combine $4^1/2$ lbs. sugar, 1 lb. corn syrup, and 1 % pints water.

Bring to boil, skimming off any foreign matter that rises to top. Boil to 246°F. Add $^1/2$ pint evaporated milk. Cook to 238°F. Pour onto cold, damp marble slab. Cream when cool.

FORMULA V

In kettle, combine 2 lbs. brown sugar, 2 lbs. maple sugar, 4 lbs. sugar, 1 1/2 lbs. corn syrup, and 1 qt. water. Stir on stove until thoroughly dissolved.

Bring to boil, skimming off any foreign matter. Boil to 238°F. Pour hot syrup onto cold, damp marble slab. Sprinkle an amount of cool water over the syrup. Allow to cool, then cream or work into maple fondant.

MELTING DOWN AND RUNNING STOCK

A copper double boiler is good for making large quantities of cream stock for casting into starch impressions. Fill larger of kettles with boiling water and smaller one with cream stock. Stir gently and constantly until the cream stock has melted. Stock containing glucose or corn syrup will require more heat to melt. Add any coloring or flavoring after stock has melted.

When using either prepared nougat or an egg, add while melting. Do not overheat or centers will be too hard. If under heated, centers may shrink, or tops may sink down. If you put your finger into the cream stock while melting, and it is hot, but does not burn your finger, it is probably ready to put into starch molds. If the cream stock begins to stiffen, it may be thinned with a little corn syrup. If the cream stock used contains corn syrup, add plain syrup for thinning.

SPECIAL NOTE: Simple syrup may be produced by combining 2 lbs. sugar and 3 pints water in a kettle. Bring quickly to a boil, about 220°F. It is then ready to use.

Lesson 86
CHOCOLATE CREAM BAR

In double boiler, melt 5 Ibs. cream stock Formula I and melt. Add 1 Ib. finely shredded coconut. Flavor lightly with vanilla and lemon extract. If extra rich bar is preferred, add 1/2 Ib. Velveeta fondant cream during melting. Cast into starch impressions using either bar or cake patterns. Allow to set up. Remove from starch and gently dust off excess starch. Coat cream centers with sweet or milk chocolate.

Lesson 87
CHOCO-MINT CREAM CARE

In double boiler, melt 5 Ibs. cream stock Formula III and flavor to taste with oil of peppermint, remembering that a little goes a long way, and too much will overpower your batch. When thoroughly melted, cast into starch impressions. Allow to harden. Lift out gently and dust off excess starch. Dip into sweet coating chocolate..

Lesson 88
CHERRY CREAM BAR

In double boiler, melt 10 Ibs. cream stock Formula II. Grind 1/2 Ib. thoroughly drained maraschino cherries. Add to melted stock. Use red coloring as desired. Use very small amount of citric acid to bring out flavor of cherries. For smoother bar, add 1 1/2 Ibs. Velveeta fondant cream. Pour melted stock into starch impressions. Allow to set up, then dip into sweet or milk

STRAWBERRY CREAM BAR

In double boiler, melt 10 Ibs. stock Formula I or Formula II. Add 1/2 Ib. crushed strawberry jam. Color red or pink, and add a little citric acid to bring out flavor. Run syrup into starch impressions. Allow to set up, and then dip in sweet or milk chocolate.

Lesson 90
PINEAPPLE CREAM BAR

Use same process as for strawberry cream bar, except substitute 1/2 Ib. crushed pineapple jam fop strawberry jam. Color batch as desired and put into starch impressions. Allow to set, then dip in sweet coating chocolate.

Lesson 91
ORANGE CREAM BAR

Use same process as for strawberry cream bar, except substitute orange jam (see below) for strawberry jam. Color batch a light orange and pour into starch impression. Allow to set, then dip in sweet chocolate.
ORANGE JAM- Grind 4 oranges. In kettle, place oranges, 1 Ib. sugar, 1/2 Ib. corn syrup, and enough water to thoroughly dissolve. Cook until mixture falls easily from spoon and becomes liquid. Other jams may be made using the same process.

Lesson 92
MAPLE WALNUT CREAM BAR

In double boiler, melt 8 Ibs. stock Formula V. Flavor with maple or use a little burnt sugar coloring (see below). Add 1 Ib. walnuts. Pour into starch impressions. Test bars about an hour after pouring to see if setting properly. Do not allow to set too long or bars will become too hard (starch will absorb all moisture from them). After the bars have set, remove from impressions and dust off excess starch.
BURNT SUGAR COLORING- In kettle, place small amount sugar. Allow to darken and burn. Remove from stove and add a little water. Mix well. Too much water will weaken the color.

Lesson 93
JELLY CREAM BARS

P lace 2 ozs. gelatin in about 3 pints water for about 1 hour. Dissolve thoroughly and strain. In kettle, place gelatin, 3 Ibs. sugar and 2 Ibs. corn syrup. Bring to boil, and stir until syrup runs off spoon in a fine stream. Remove from stove and allow to cool. While waiting, strain and mash into a sieve the fruit to be made into jam. To fruit pulp add 1/2 Ib. sugar and 4 ozs. corn syrup. Cook to heavy syrup. Add a little citric acid and mix well. When thick enough, pour into warm starch impressions, using bar molds, filling molds only 1/3 full. Let set overnight. Melt down about 8 Ibs. stock Formula III and flavor with vanilla. Using funnel, run cream stock to fill starch impressions rest of the way. Allow to set up. Finish by dipping in sweet or milk

VANILLA CREAM BAR

I n double boiler, melt a quantity of stock Formula I, II, or II. Flavor to taste with vanilla. Run mixture into starch impressions. Allow to set up. Remove them and dust off any excess starch stuck to bars. Coat in either sweet or milk chocolate.

Lesson 95
CHOCOLATE FUDGE BAR

In double boiler, melt a quantity stock Formula I, Formula II, or Formula III. Add grated bitter chocolate while melting. Amount of chocolate depends on whether light or dark chocolate is desired. Be sure stock is soft, as chocolate will thicken it considerably.

Lesson 96
FRUIT FUDGE BAR

In double boiler, melt 5 Ibs. stock Formula IV. Add 1/4 Ib. candied cherries, ^/4 Ib. seedless raisins, and 1A Ib. chopped citron. Add 1/2 Ib. Velveeta fondant cream if desired. Mix well and pour or run into starch impressions. Allow to set, then coat with sweet or milk chocolate.

Lesson 97 NUT FUDGE BAR

Proceed as for fruit fudge bar, except add 3/4 Ib. assorted chopped nuts instead of fruit. For chocolate flavor, add 1/2 Ib. melted bitter chocolate.

Lesson 98
CHOCOLATE SURPRISE ROLL

With hands, thoroughly knead 4 Ibs. stock Formula III. Work in 2 Ibs. good quality peanut butter. Form into little rolls, about 2" long and 11/2" thick. Place on tray covered with waxed paper until firm enough to handle.

Meanwhile, cook a batch of caramel. In kettle, place 31/2 Ibs. corn syrup, 3 Ibs. sugar, 2 1/2 lbs. condensed milk, and 6 ozs. paraffin substitute. Stir on stove until thoroughly dissolve. Stir constantly to prevent scorching. Cook to 245°F. Quickly remove from stove. Add 1 t. salt and 1/2 oz. vanilla. Set kettle containing caramel mixture on a work table.

Place blanched peanuts on cold, greased marble slab. With large fork, dip peanut cream rolls into hot caramel and quickly remove. Roll balls in blanched peanuts on slab. (Use plenty of peanuts.) Place on another slightly greased slab and allow to cool. When cool, dip into sweet or milk chocolate. SPECIAL NOTE: If caramel minutes to soften. Don't becomes stiff before finishing, place back on stove for a few cover centers with an excessive amount of caramel

CARAMEL BAR

In kettle, place 5 Ibs. sugar, 3 1/2 Ibs. corn syrup, and 2 qts. condensed milk. Stir on stove until boiling point is reached, then add 4 ozs. paraffin substitute. Boil to 245°F, stirring constantly to prevent scorching. (Too high a temperature will result in a product that is hard and tough.) Remove from stove and flavor to taste with vanilla. If desired, add 1 1/2 Ibs. finely grated bitter chocolate. Allow to cool, then pour or run into starch impressions, using funnel and stick, as in casting cream stock. When filling impressions, sprinkle a little starch over tops of centers. Allow centers to set up. When ready to handle, coat with sweet chocolate.

Lesson 100 NOUGAT BAR

In double boiler, melt 5 Ibs. stock Formula I. Cook to 240°F-242°F (instead of 238°F) because larger part of nougat cream is added later when stock has melted. Add 2 Ibs. Velveeta nougat cream. Flavor and color as desired. Run nougat into starch bar impressions and allow to set overnight. Remove and dip into sweet or milk chocolate.

Lesson 101
PECAN NOUGAT ROLL

In kettle, place 2 Ibs. sugar, 1/2 Ib. corn syrup, and 1/2 pint water. Cook to 256°F-258°F. Remove from stove. Add 12 oz. Velveeta nougat cream, 1/2 Ib. smooth cream stock, 1 oz. shaved paraffin substitute, and a quantity of chopped nuts. Mix and beat. Pour onto slab lightly sprinkled with confectioner's sugar. Allow to cool, then form into rolls of desired size. Rolls are ready to dip.

In another kettle, place 1 Ib. sugar, 1 Ib. corn syrup, 1 Ib. Velveeta caramel cream, 1 pint condensed milk, and 4 ozs. paraffin substitute. Add enough water to dissolve. Boil to 246°F. With wire candy dipper, or using two forks, dip nougat rolls into hot caramel. Roll in ground pecan nuts. Place on slightly greased slab to harden. May be sliced if you desire.

MARSHMALLOW PEANUT BAR

Dissolve 4 ozs. granulated gelatin in 1 1/2 pints lukewarm water and set aside. In kettle, place 5 Ibs. sugar, 3 1/2 Ibs. Corn syrup and 1 pint water. Stir on stove until thoroughly dissolved. Cook to 240°F. Remove from stove and add prepared gelatin water. Beat with wooden paddle or spatula until light and white. (The more you beat this marshmallow batch, the better it becomes.) Color and flavor as desired. Run into warm starch bar impressions. Dust small amount starch over each impression as it is filled. Use double boiler to keep marshmallow soft enough to run through funnel. If marshmallow becomes too thick, thin by adding a quantity of simple syrup (see Lesson 86). Allow centers to set enough to be removed and finished.

Coat with sweet or milk chocolate. Before chocolate completely hardens, scatter well-blanched, chopped, roasted peanuts or shredded coconut over tops.

Lesson 103
MARSHMALLOW CARAMEL CREAM BAR

Take a batch of marshmallow peanut bar, as previously described. Fill starch impressions a little over half. Allow to set overnight in impressions.

Cook a caramel batch to fill impressions rest of way. In kettle, place 4 Ibs. sugar, 3 Ibs. corn syrup, 1 qt. fresh cream, and 2 ozs. paraffin substitute. Stir on stove until thoroughly dissolved. Boil to about 230°F. Add 1 additional qt. cream and cook to 245°F. Remove from stove. Flavor to taste with vanilla. Allow to cool somewhat. While still a little warm, run into impressions previously half-filled with marshmallow. Dust a little starch over each impression to prevent stickiness. Allow to set. Coat with sweet or milk
chocolate.

Lesson 104 ORIENT BAR

In kettle, place 4 1/2 Ibs. corn syrup, 1 Ib. sugar, and 1 pint water. Cook to soft ball stage, or about 240°F. In another kettle, place 9 Ibs. finely shredded coconut. Slowly pour hot syrup over coconut, working coconut into syrup with paddle or spatula. Mix well until a thick paste. Flavor and color as desired. Pour onto cold, slightly greased slab. Roll out thinly and allow to remain an hour or so. Cut into bars and roll in granulated sugar.

Lesson 105
BUTTERSCOTCH CREAM BAR

In kettle, place 3 Ibs. corn syrup, 21/2 Ibs. sugar, 2 ozs. paraffin substitute, and 1/2 pint water. Stir until thoroughly dissolved. Cook to 260°F. Add 1 Ib. condensed milk and 4 ozs. butter. Boil to 245°F. Remove from stove. Add 1 t. salt and allow to cool. Run into starch impressions, filling only half full. Melt a quantity of stock Formula III. Flavor and color as desired. Use to finish filling impressions. Allow to set. Dip in sweet or milk chocolate.

PISTACHIO CREAM BAR

In kettle, melt 5 Ibs. stock Formula I. Add 1 Ib. Velveeta fondant cream or similar product. Color green. Flavor with pistachio and add 1/2 Ib. pistachio nuts. Run into starch bar impressions. Allow to set. Dip in sweet or milk chocolate.

Lesson 107
COFFEE CREAM BAR

In kettle, melt 5 Ibs. stock Formula III or Formula IV. Use burnt sugar (see Lesson 92) to give a coffee color. Use coffee flavoring (see Lesson 81) if desired. When cream is right consistency, pour into starch bar impressions.
Allow to set. Remove from starch and dust off excess. Coat in sweet chocolate.

Lesson 108
PLANTATIONS

In kettle, place 4 Ibs. sugar, 3 Ibs. corn syrup, 2 ozs. paraffin substitute, and 1 pint water. Stir on stove until thoroughly dissolved. Boil to 250°F. Add 1 pint high quality molasses and 4 oz. butter. Cook to 246°F. Remove from stove. Allow to cool to about 139°F. Run batch through funnel into starch
impressions. For this type candy, do not use large molds, but, instead, use molds about the size used for caramels. Allow centers to set. Remove from molds and coat with sweet chocolate.

Lesson 109
CHOCOLATE WHIPPED CREAMS

In double boiler, place 12 Ibs. stock Formula III. Melt slowly. In a different kettle, place 3 Ibs. sugar, 2 Ibs. corn syrup, and 1 pint water. Cook and boil to 236°F. Pour into melted stock. Add 1 1/2 Ibs. Velveeta fondant cream. Flavor and color as desired. Pour or run into starch impressions.

Allow to set overnight. Remove from impressions and coat with sweet or milk chocolate.

Lesson 110 TURKISH DELIGHT

SPECIAL NOTE: Experimentation and patience is called for when making this candy since you will not be able to successfully use your thermometer. If the batch is not cooked enough, it will be too soft. If cooked too long, it will be tough and may scorch. The most popular flavors for this candy are lemon, orange, and raspberry.

Dissolve 8 oz. corn starch in 8 oz. cold water and set aside. In kettle, place 5 Ibs. sugar and 1 qt. water. Bring to boil. Add dissolved corn starch. Stir on stove until mixture begins to thicken. Add 3 Ibs. corn syrup. Continue stirring until begins to boil, then add a pinch of cream of tartar. Cook until a heavy jelly-like substance. Flavor and color as desired. Pour onto tray (preferably wooden) lined with waxed paper. Sprinkle with a combination of half confectioner's sugar and half corn starch. Dust top of candy with same combination. Allow to set for two days before removing. May be sliced, or left in 1 Ib. chunks.

CHOP SUEY BAR

In kettle, place 4 Ibs. sugar, 2 Ibs. corn syrup, 1 1/2 ozs. paraffin substitute, and 1 pint water. Stir on stove until thoroughly dissolved. Cook to 248°F. Add 3 1/2 Ibs. raw, shelled Spanish peanuts. Stir constantly to prevent scorching. After adding peanuts, thermometer will not register accurately. Use cold water test to determine stage of candy. Cook until peanuts are well roasted and syrup breaks brittle when tested in cold water. Add 1 1/4 Ibs. coconut, 1 T. bicarbonate, and 1 T. salt. Mix well (especially soda) into batch. Quickly pour onto greased marble slab. Spread very thinly. Before candy hardens, cut into bar shapes.

Lesson 112 NUT BAR

In kettle, place 3 Ibs. sugar, 2 Ibs. corn syrup, and 1 pint water or enough water to thoroughly dissolve while stirring on stove. Cook to 248°F. Add 4 Ibs. mixed nuts and 1 t. salt. Pour onto greased marble slab. Spread thinly. Before candy hardens, cut into bar shapes. Wrap in either tinfoil or waxed paper.

Lesson 113 MONTEROSA BAR

In kettle, place 2 Ibs. sugar, 2 Ibs. corn syrup, 2 Ibs. condensed milk, and 2 1/2 ozs. paraffin substitute. Dissolve in a little water. Stir constantly on stove, boiling to 248°F, or to hard ball stage. Add 2 Ibs. plain cream stock or stock Formula I, 1 Ibs. corn syrup, 1 Ib. shaved milk chocolate, and 1 Ib. chopped almonds. Flavor with vanilla. Add 1 t. salt. Mix and beat thoroughly, then pour onto tray (preferably wood) lined with waxed paper. If too hard to handle, soften in double boiler. When cool, cut into bars in desired sizes.

Lesson 114
MEXICAN PRALINES

Formula 1:

In kettle, place 2 1/2 Ibs. brown sugar with enough water to thoroughly dissolve. Add 1/4 t. cream of tartar, and boil to 242°F. Do not stir after coming to a boil. At 242°F, remove from stove and add 4 ozs. smooth cream stock. Mix and stir until cloudy in appearance, and some grain is seen in batch. Onto waxed paper or wooden trays lined with waxed paper, spoon into small cake-shaped pieces, about 4" in diameter. Mixture may be thinned, if needed, by placing back in kettle to soften. Before cakes harden completely, place 6 to 8 pecan halves on top of cakes.

Formula 2:

In kettle, place 2 Ibs. brown sugar, 2 Ibs. maple sugar, 12 ozs. corn syrup, and 1 1/2 pints water. Boil on stove to 240°F. Add 1/4 Ib. cream stock and 2 Ibs. pecan halves. Allow to cool 3 minutes. Stir and mix with spatula, then spoon onto waxed paper in cake-shaped pieces, about 4" in diameter.

Lesson 115
CHOCOLATE COCONUT DELIGHTS

Make cream stock or fondant by mixing 3 Ibs. sugar, 1/2 Ib. corn syrup, and 1 pint water. Boil to 238°F. Pour syrup onto cold, damp slab. Sprinkle with 6 ozs. grated bitter chocolate. When cooled, cream using paddle or
spatula. Allow to set 1 hour to ripen. Melt in double boiler as for casting in starch. When completely melted, add 1/2 Ib. coconut and 2 ozs. butter. Mix thoroughly. Mix or cream with spatula. Spoon onto waxed paper-lined trays into kisses or other shapes. Chocolate may be replaced with other flavors for variety.

Lesson 116
ROYAL PENOCHE

In kettle, place 2 Ibs. brown sugar, 2 Ibs. maple sugar, 1 Ib. corn syrup, and 1 pint water. Stir on stove until thoroughly dissolved. Cook to 240°F. Remove from stove. Allow to cool about 2 minutes. Add 5 Ibs. plain cream stock or stock Formula I. Thoroughly mix and work into warm syrup. Add 1
t. salt, 1 T. vanilla, 2 oz. glycerin, and 3 1/2 Ibs. nuts, preferably pecans. Mix together and pour onto tray lined with waxed paper.

Lesson 117
SCOTCH KISSES

Set aside package of marshmallows, or marshmallows you have made. In kettle, place 5 Ibs. cane sugar, 1 Ib. corn syrup, and 1 1/2 pints water. Dissolve thoroughly and boil to 300°F. Add 3 ozs. butter. Boil again to 300°F. Remove from stove. With wire candy dipper or large fork, dip marshmallow into butterscotch syrup, removing quickly. Place marshmallow on slightly greased slab. If syrup thickens, set back on stove to soften.

Lesson 118
DIXIE PRIZE BAR

In kettle, place 4 Ibs. sugar, 1 Ib. corn syrup, and 1 pint water. Stir thoroughly and boil. Add 4 Ibs. shelled, roasted Spanish peanuts. Stir a little and cook to 244°F-246°F. Remove from stove. Stir until grainy and cloudy in appearance. Pour onto slightly greased slab. Cool and cut into bars.

SEASIDE CHEWING KISSES

In kettle, place 5 Ibs. sugar, 6 Ibs. corn syrup, 3 ozs. butter, 4 ozs. hard nut butter, or another paraffin substitute, and 1 pint water. Stir until dissolved and cook to 260°F. Pour onto cold, greased marble slab. Sprinkle 1 T. salt over candy while cooling. When cool, place on candy hook and pull thoroughly. Flavor and color as desired. Do not pull when still warm, or candy may slide off hook. When nice and light, place on table which has been dusted with 1/3 confectioner's sugar and 2/3 corn starch. Spin or shape into rope shape. Clip or cut into kisses shapes. Wrap in colored waxed paper.

Popular flavors are lemon, lime, molasses. Molasses kisses are made by adding 1/2 pint molasses after batch has been cooked to 256°F, then following remaining instructions.

vanilla, chocolate, strawberry, anise, sassafras, and

Lesson 120

CANADIAN BUTTER TOFFEE

In kettle, place 1 1/4 Ibs. sugar, 1 Ib. corn syrup, 4 ozs. sweet cream, 3 ozs. butter, and 8 ozs. fresh evaporated milk. Stir on stove to thoroughly dissolve. Cook, stirring constantly, to 246°F. Remove from stove and allow to cool until lukewarm. Flavor with 1 T. vanilla. Pour about 3/4" thick onto cold, slightly greased marble slab. When completely cold, cut into squares and wrap in waxed paper.

Lesson 121 BUTTERCUPS

In kettle, place 5 Ibs. sugar, 1/2 t. cream of tartar, and 1 qt. water. Stir until thoroughly dissolved, washing down inside walls of kettle. Boil to 335°F. Pour onto greased slab. While cooling, fold together. When cool enough to handle, put on candy hook and pull until glossy. Add a little vanilla while pulling. Twist air from batch. Place on table near stove and flatten to 10"-12" wide. This batch makes the outside jacket for all kinds of buttercups. **Lesson 122**

CREAM BUTTERCUPS

In double boiler, melt 2 Ibs. cream stock. Add a few drops vanilla and 2- 3 ozs. butter. Dissolve butter thoroughly. Add enough confectioner's sugar to stiffen. On table, place flattened buttercup jacket made in Lesson 121. Place cream buttercup formula on jacket. Roll jacket into sticks about the size of your finger and cut into short pieces.

PEANUT BUTTER CUPS
Prepare jacket as in Lesson 121. Make cream buttercups, adding peanut butter.

Lesson 124
ALL-DAY SUCKERS
During warm weather, it is advisable to use the second of the following formulas. Good, clear days are good for making this candy. On cool damp days, candy may become sticky. Formula 1:
In kettle, place 4 Ibs. sugar, 1 Ib. corn syrup, and about 1 1/2 pints water. Stir until dissolved. Cook to 300°F.
Formula 2:
In kettle, place 4 Ibs. sugar, 1/4 t. cream of tartar, and 1 pint water. Stir until dissolved. Do not stir after batch begins to boil. Wash down inside walls of kettle. Cook to 330°F.

When either batch has reached boiling point, quickly remove from stove and pour onto greased slab. Turn in edges. Knead in 1 T. powdered citric acid and desired flavoring. Form into paste. Add coloring, then knead again. Spin or shape into rope and cut or clip pieces. Insert sticks for suckers. Or, run mixture through funnel into slightly greased molds. Lift out just before cold and insert sticks. Return to molds to harden.

Lesson 125
MAKING CANDY CANES
Formula 1:
In kettle, place 6 Ibs. sugar, 1 1/2 Ibs. Corn syrup, and 1 qt. water. Dissolve on stove. Cook to 300°F-310°F.
Formula 2:
In kettle, place 5 Ibs. sugar, 1/2 t. cream of tartar, and 1 1/2 pints water. Dissolve on stove. Cook to 320°F.

Pour syrup of either formula onto well-greased marble slab. Fold in corners with a knife. When cool enough to handle, cut off small piece and color deep red. Knead color in with hands and place near stove or in batch warmer to keep soft. Take remaining, larger piece and place on candy hook. Pull until white and shiny. Add a few drops oil of peppermint while pulling. (Wear clean latex or rubber gloves to avoid burning hands.) Twist air from batch and place on table near stove or batch warmer. Form into loaf shape. Roll red piece into strips about finger thickness. Make 4 red strips and place lengthwise on larger, white candy loaf.

Continued from page 53

Roll loaf until round, pressing harder on one end than the other. Twist and spin candy into stick sizes about middle finger size. Make a crook or hook shape at one end, bending into shape before candy becomes cold. When hardened, it will retain this shape.

Lesson 126 LEMON DROPS

SPECIAL NOTE: Work fast when making this candy so it will not become too cold or hard. It is good to have a batch warmer on hand.

Make citric acid paste by adding 1 t. oil of lemon or 1 T. lemon extract to powdered citric acid. (Use oil for more prominent flavor.) Set aside.

In kettle, place 7 1/2 lbs. sugar, 1 qt. water, and 1/2 t. cream of tartar. Stir on stove to dissolve. Wash down inside walls of kettle. Boil to about 330°F. Pour onto greased slab. Fold in edges. When cool enough to handle, knead in 1/2 oz. citric acid paste. Cut into drop pieces. When drops have hardened, dampen and roll in sugar. Pack in glass jars.

Orange, wild cherry, lime, or raspberry drops may be produced using the same formula. Substitute these or other colors and flavors and add to the citric acid.

Lesson 127
FRENCH CHEWING CANDY

Dissolve 1 oz. granulated gelatin in 1/2 pint water and set aside. In kettle, place 7 lbs. sugar, 4 lbs. corn syrup, and 1 qt. water. Stir on stove until thoroughly dissolved. Stirring continually, add 1/2 pint condensed milk, 1 oz. cocoa butter, and 1/2 lb. butter. Boil to 265°F. Pour onto greased slab.

Sprinkle gelatin water over surface of hot candy syrup. Fold in edges. Allow cool enough to handle. Put on candy hook and pull until light. Add flavor and color as desired while pulling. Dust with a little corn starch. Shape into large, round batch, and place in pan lined with white muslin. Allow to harden and break off pieces to any size.

Lesson 128
SALT WATER KISSES

In kettle, place 3 Ibs. crystal white corn syrup, 2 1/2 Ibs. sugar, 2 oz. paraffin substitute, and 1 1/2 pints water. Stir on stove until thoroughly dissolved. Cook to 256°F-258°F. Pour onto greased slab. Fold in edges and allow to cool. When cool enough to handle, put on candy hook and pull until extremely light and bulky. Work in 2 t. salt while pulling. Add desired flavors and colors while pulling. On table, twist or spin into rope shape and cut into kisses. Wrap in waxed paper.

www.ingramcontent.com/pod-product-compliance
Lightning Source LLC
LaVergne TN
LVHW042321190525
811730LV00039B/990